Wedding Ceremonies Made Easy

Vows, Readings, Traditions, Officiant Questions, and More!

Dr. Rev. Cheryl Q

ISBN:148275357X
ISBN-13:9781482753578

DEDICATION

To those who have found their soul mate….

May You Always Be Each Other's Best Friend and
Greatest Love

CONTENTS

Introduction

About the Book Author

INTRODUCTION

As a Wedding Officiant, I have the best job in the world. I get to be there when you begin your married life. When I first meet you, you are two people with a dream of forever; when I leave you, your lives are forever changed because of one word – Married. It's exciting and it's the best. What is included in the following pages is what I have learned and gathered through the years from my clients. This information is being shared with you as an educational resource, in hopes that it will help guide you through an important part of the most special day in your lives. As an added bonus, I've included two articles I wrote about how to hire a DJ and using MP3 players vs. DJ's. Let your celebration begin!

1
CEREMONIES

Let's talk for a minute about wedding ceremonies. This is the special time when your family and friends gather to see you united as Husband and Wife. Ceremonies never used to be as elaborate as they are now. Most ceremonies were small affairs performed at home with a few family members, and maybe friends, present. During the early times, the bride generally had one good dress, which was the one she was married in. It wasn't unusual for her to get married in black or brown or grey. Queen Victoria is credited with wearing white when she got married in the mid-1800s and the color caught on, first in England and then in the United States.

There are generally two types of ceremonies: created ceremonies, or generic ceremonies that are 'cookie-cutter.' In 'cookie-cutter' ceremonies, the officiant reads from a generic script and just plugs in your names. An example of this would be weddings performed in Las Vegas or on a cruise ship. In created ceremonies, the officiant works to incorporate your personality into the ceremony. This can be done through personalized vows, selected readings, family or friends' participation, etc.

Wedding Ceremonies traditionally consist of at least five main parts: The Opening, the Intent, the Vows, the Ring Exchange, and the Closing/Pronouncement. Other areas may be added, such as the Giving Away of the Bride and Readings. Nothing is really considered 'traditional' these days, so you can add in or take out what you want. However, the following is how a wedding ceremony usually flows.

The Opening – This is the welcoming of guests. Probably the most familiarly known is: "We are gathered here today to join this man and woman in Matrimony."

The Intent – Basically, the officiant is asking if you are here of your own free will.

Giving Away of Bride – Can be done here or in the beginning before the Opening remarks. The difference is that whoever is giving away the bride will be standing longer. If it's done earlier, the bride will be handed over immediately; if it's done later, the officiant should ask, "Who gives this woman in marriage?"

Readings and Comments – The time to talk about marriage and its importance. A favorite poem or reading could be inserted here. You are not limited to only one reading. Another reading can easily be added at this point, or before the blessing/wishes. Just remember, your guests are sitting or standing so try and keep the readings short.

The Vows – There are many options of writing your own vows, or selecting vows which are generally repeated after the officiant. If you are composing your own vows, write them down, send a copy to your officiant, and take a copy with you to read. You will be naturally nervous and your emotions might get the best of you, so avoid an awkward moment and write them down.

The Ring Exchange – Can be a dual or single ring ceremony. Sometimes is combined with the vows. Usually, however, is a separate portion that is repeated after the officiant, where you place a ring on each other's fourth finger of the left hand (where the 'vein of love' resides.) HINT: typically the bride's left hand is on officiant's side; the groom's left hand is on guests' side.

Ceremonies within Ceremony – Sand Ceremonies, Unity Candles, Butterfly Releases, Wishing Stones, or Rose Ceremonies would be added here.

Blessing or Wishes – Either ask God to bless your ceremony or ask guests to join in wishing the best for the couple.

The Closing and Pronouncement – Usually, "by the authority vested in me, I now pronounce you man and wife."

Many couples elect to include various readings and/or little ceremonies within the ceremony, such as the Unity Candle or Sand Ceremony. These are explained a little later in the book.

Don't Panic! Most ceremonies are simple: you repeat after the officiant or answer a question, so there is very little, if anything, to memorize. If you are doing your own vows, it is strongly advised to write them down and send a copy to your officiant. Even the best and most prepared speakers get nervous. **Don't attempt to 'wing it.'**

Of course, part of the ceremony is also the Processional, or how you make it down the aisle! Here are a few things to remember about the Processional:

- Traditionally, the Bridesmaids go left; Groomsmen go right.
- Brides usually walk on the left side of whoever will be giving her away.
- Flowers are held navel-high. HINT: Thumb knuckle in the navel will keep the flowers where they are supposed to be held.
- Remember to smile!
- Maid of Honor holds Groom's ring.
- Best Man holds Bride's ring.

This is YOUR Wedding. If you want to dance down the aisle, then go ahead and do it! It might be best to let your officiant know, so they can perfect their moves and join in.....

2
VOWS

Wedding vows are the most public and most personal legal steps you will take in your lifetime of dedication to each other. Whether you use these examples of wedding vows or come up with your own, the vow's intent is to express your love and commitment, and to publicly declare to your guests and the world that, as a couple, you are pledging your lives to each other. If you choose to create your own vows, write them down and make sure your officiant has a copy well in advance. **Do not attempt to 'wing it.'** (Yes, I'm repeating myself.).

The following are a few sample examples of wedding vows that are favorites of my clients. Many others are available on the Internet.

I, (Bride/Groom), take you (Groom/Bride), to be my (wife/husband), to have and to hold from this day forward, for better or for worse, for richer, for poorer, in sickness and in health, to love and to cherish; from this day forward until death do us part.

I, (name), take you (name), to be my (husband/wife), my partner in life and my one true love. I will cherish our union and love you more each day than I did the day before. I will trust you and respect you, laugh with you and cry with you, loving you faithfully through good times and bad, regardless of the obstacles we may face together. I give you my hand, my heart, and my love, from this day forward for as long as we both shall live.

I, (name), take you (name), to be my friend, my lover, the (mother/father) of my children and my (husband/wife). I will be yours in times of plenty and in times of want, in times of sickness and in times of health, in times of joy and in times of sorrow, in times of failure and in times of triumph.

I promise to cherish and respect you, to care and protect you, to comfort and encourage you, and stay with you, for all eternity.

I, (name), choose you (name), to be my (husband/wife), to respect you in your successes and in your failures, to care for you in sickness and in health, to nurture you, and to grow with you throughout the seasons of life.

FOR THE GROOM: I, (name), take you (name), to be my partner in life. I promise to walk by your side forever and to love, help, and encourage you in all that you do.

I will take time to talk with you, to listen to you, and to care for you. I will share your laughter and your tears as your partner, lover, and best friend. Everything I am and everything I have is yours now and forevermore.

FOR THE BRIDE: I, (name), give myself to you (name), on this our wedding day.

I will cherish our friendship and love you today, tomorrow, and forever. I will trust you and honor you. I will love you faithfully through the best and the worst, through the difficult and the easy.

Whatever comes our way, I will be there always. As I have given you my hand to hold so I give you my life to keep.

In some weddings, after the solitary vows, the bride and groom recite a vow in unison while lighting a unity candle or doing a sand ceremony. This re-enforces the public commitment, as well as providing an extra reference for the guests. It's also the first public act the couple completes in a formal, recognized, committed partnership.

3

QUESTIONS TO ASK YOUR OFFICIANT

How soon should couples book their date with a wedding officiant? As with any vendor, wedding officiants should be booked as soon as possible. Good officiants are generally booked 9 months to a year or more in advance. Special dates, such as Valentine's Day, New Year's Eve, New Year's Day, or dates such as 11/11/11, 12/12/12, 11/12/13, etc. are popular and book up fast. If you know you are getting married and want a particular officiant, it would be advantageous to book early.

What are customary policies regarding deposits? Policies vary from officiant to officiant. Most require a deposit ranging from 25-50% with full payment 7-14 days in advance. It is advisable to work with an officiant who will give you an agreement or contract in writing. This adds legitimacy to who you are hiring, and also gives you legal backing should something go wrong. In addition to an agreement, your officiant should have insurance.

Is it typical for couples to meet with the wedding officiant prior to the wedding? It depends on the officiant. Many don't meet the couple prior to the wedding. Some meet with the couple to plan their ceremony after a deposit is made. Generally, this meeting includes talking about vows, readings, the ceremony in general, and ideas for anything special they might like to have included, such as a ceremony within a ceremony, i.e. candle lighting, sand ceremony, etc. This meeting is 1-2 hours. Some wedding sites recommend interviewing the officiant for 'compatibility,' prior to booking. Most officiants don't like interviews, mainly because these are generally not a good use of time. Other than saying, "hello," little useful information is exchanged in comparison to after an officiant is booked.

If a bride and groom are of different faiths, or one of them is not religious, is that a problem? For me, no; however, there could be some issues with some faiths, so it's a good idea to check with the officiant and ask during the initial call. As all my ceremonies are created instead of 'canned,' the couple has a lot of leeway for what they want. They can have faith-based traditions included, and as much or as little religion as they would like. During the planning process, family sensitivities are discussed and the ceremony is created so as to respect the faiths of both families.

If the bride and/or the groom was married before, but is now legally divorced, will a wedding officiant marry them? Some religions don't recognize a second marriage or divorce, so there may or may not be a problem. This should be discussed with the officiant beforehand, especially if the officiant is a minister, priest, or rabbi. There generally are no problems with divorced individuals in Civil Ceremonies.

Can children be incorporated into the vows? It is highly recommended and encouraged that children be involved as much as possible. Children are a part of the marriage of two people, and should be a part of the ceremony so they don't feel left out. I have a family ceremony that is beautiful, where I join not only the couple as husband and wife, but I join the couple and the children as a new family.

Does the wedding officiant normally go to the rehearsal? There is generally a fee for the rehearsal that is charged by almost every officiant. It's up to the couple as to whether or not they want to spend the money. I have gone to rehearsals. But conversely, have provided enough information during the planning meeting so this money can be spent elsewhere. In reality, most people have already gone to a wedding or been in a wedding. The rehearsal is mainly to show the bridal party how to line up, walk down the aisle, and where to stand. A family member or friend, or officiants who are more 'hands on,' might be able to help with this on the day of the wedding.

How long does the wedding officiant normally stay after the ceremony? Officiants normally should depart after the license is signed. If there are activities such as photos where the officiant is needed, he/she should stay. Unless invited to stay for the cocktail hour or reception, the officiant should not be there, nor should they expect to be invited. An officiant is 'hired' to perform a service, which is the ceremony, and meals are expensive. I personally think it is tacky for an officiant not only to partake in the celebration of family and friends when meals are so expensive, but I've even seen them bring a spouse or date.

Does the wedding officiant wear a traditional robe or do they dress in other attire? Some officiants offer the couple a choice as to whether they want a traditional robe, or attire in keeping with the wedding such as formal, business, casual, beach, theme, etc. while others do not.

How much are couples typically allowed to customize the ceremony? There are officiants who show up and start reading from a book. In that case, there is little to no customization allowed. When a ceremony is personalized, there is a lot of room for self-expression. From vow selections and readings, to anything special a couple might want such as a Dr. Seuss verse or something from Star Wars, or even honoring a deceased parent, it's their wedding; and my feeling is, they should be allowed to customize the ceremony.

Do wedding officiants allow couples to write their own vows? Some officiants either give their couples a list from which to choose, or offer no selection whatsoever. I not only allow couples to write their own vows, but encourage them to do so. There have been a couple of cases where one or the other has had trouble expressing themselves and I've actually written the vows for them or helped in writing them.

Will wedding officiants generally marry couples that are not members of a religious congregation? This depends on the officiant. Couples who want a religious connection in their marriage, yet do not belong to a religious congregation, should look for a non-denominational minister. A Civil Ceremony is another option.

Are friends allowed to participate in the ceremony, including giving readings, singing, or anything else? How should these things be coordinated with the wedding officiant? It always makes a ceremony more special when family or friends are involved. There are many ways to incorporate them, too. Have them light the first initial candles in a unity candle ceremony, or have different colors of sand in containers that are poured into one container, representing the families. Many people are not good public speakers, so if a friend or family member is going to read, a little practice beforehand is recommended. In all cases, the officiant should be told beforehand.

How much do wedding officiants usually charge for services? $250-$750

Are there additional charges? Some officiants charge more for inclusion of ceremonies within your ceremony, such as sand ceremony or unity candle, or for the number of people present. There may be an additional charge if your ceremony starts late (generally 15-30 minutes after the contracted time). It is customary to pay for any parking fees incurred by the officiant.

Do I need to tip the officiant? Tipping has always been a personal expression of gratitude for service given and appreciated. First, an important reminder, that gratuities are always, always discretionary (optional) tokens of appreciation for service that exceeds expectations. No professional should expect a gratuity, and all should be grateful, regardless of size.

If your officiant is charging for the service, then tip 15%-25% if you feel their service was exceptional. The average gratuity or donation for those in public service (Judge, Justice of the Peace), was between $50 and $100.

If a member of the clergy is marrying you free of charge, a donation of $75 - $100 to their church is appreciated. A paid Clergymen, Rabbi, or Priest officiant gratuity is generally $50-$75.

An additional gratuity is appreciated and almost expected if travel is involved

4

CEREMONY TYPES

A **civil ceremony** is a beautiful ceremony that doesn't reference God or any other spiritual deity. Civil ceremonies may have traditional or contemporary readings and there are no prayers or blessings. Wishes for the couple can be made instead. These ceremonies usually are performed by a Judge, Justice of the Peace, or a Clerk of the Court. Some states give marrying authority to Notaries.

A **non-denominational ceremony** is perfect for couples preferring to be married by a minister instead of a civil servant. It is typically Christian, without adhering to any particular denomination

(Catholic, Baptist, etc.) A non-denominational ceremony may or may not have traditional, Christian and/or contemporary readings, and may or may not reference God directly.

A **spiritual ceremony** is a beautiful ceremony that often incorporates traditions, blessings, and/or prayers of non-Christian faiths, i.e. Muslim or Buddhist.

Interfaith/intercultural ceremonies incorporate traditions, blessing, and/or prayers from more than one faith or culture, i.e. Buddhist and Christian elements, African and Hispanic cultures, or Christian and Jewish traditions.

A **commitment ceremony** is often very similar to many other kinds of weddings. It is not a legally binding ceremony but instead it is simply a public affirmation of a couple's commitment to one another. Generally, but not always, the couple is unable to marry under the law or chooses to not be married. Depending on the Officiant and the couple's preference, a commitment ceremony may be religious or secular, and may also be formal and traditional, or loose and unstructured.

5

CEREMONIES WITHIN YOUR CEREMONY

Unity Candle Ceremony

The Unity Candle Ceremony consists of the lighting of one candle from two separate candles, usually held by the bride and groom. This ceremony symbolizes the union of two lives into one. Sometimes the mothers of the bride and groom, children, or any designated member of the wedding party, light the candles after they walk down the aisle or during the ceremony. In Family

Ceremonies, there can be candles for not only the Bride and Groom but for each of the children. Everyone lights their candle, then lights the main candle signifying the joining of lives into one family. The couple keeps the candle (some re-light the candle each year on their anniversary). It is not recommended for outdoor ceremonies. HINT: Remember to have matches or flame lighters on the table near the candles. Don't wait until the last minute to put them there.

The Blessing of the Rings

The wedding ring is the visible sign of an inward bond which unites two loyal hearts in endless love. It is a seal of the vows made to one another. It symbolizes living together in unity, love, and happiness for the rest of their lives. Before being placed on the fingers, the rings are blessed, asking for an eternity of love and devotion.

Breaking of the Glass

The breaking of the glass at the end of a wedding ceremony usually is reserved for Jewish ceremonies. However, it is a beautiful ending to any wedding. It symbolizes that the marriage will be as difficult to dissolve as it would be to put the glass back together again. HINT: A wrapped light bulb, instead of a glass, is generally preferred as it is easier to break.

Sand Ceremony

This beautiful ceremony takes sand from two separate containers and mixes it into one container, and symbolizes two lives coming together as one. The words in this ceremony are beautiful and touching. Have your container engraved as a keepsake, use different colored sand, or even add some seashells for a beach wedding. As your guests are a part of your lives, a variation is to give your guests small bottles of sand they can add to the main container. These can be different colors. In Family Ceremonies, children can also be given sand to add to the main container.

Wishing Stones/Starfish

There are two variations of this. For Beach Weddings, give each guest a stone/starfish, either before or during the ceremony. At some point during the ceremony, usually at the end, the guests make a wish for the bride and groom and throw the stones/starfish into the water. For indoor weddings, guests can make a wish, or even write on the stone, and deposit them in a basket or container for the bride and groom to keep.

Children/Family Services

Many couples are remarrying and want to include their children in the ceremony. There are numerous ways this may be done. The Family Medallion Ceremony, a small gift for the children, or a special unity candle or sand ceremony is some ways this can be done.

Flower Ceremony

This is a family/friends ceremony and gets everyone involved. Each person or designated person comes up and places a different flower in a vase to create a garden of love. The vase can then be moved to the Bride and Grooms table or the guest sign in area. It makes a nice keepsake.

Honoring the Mothers

A brief reading is done and then the bride and groom together present their mother(s) with a small gift (flowers, usually). If you choose to give your mothers a rose, the florist can quietly add a couple to the bridal bouquet, so it will be a complete surprise to the moms.

Silent Blessing and Moment of Remembrance

Both are small blessings/readings honoring the deceased. They may include specific names or a general statement. This should be tastefully done, both to honor the deceased and still keep the wedding as a celebration. It is preferred this is done earlier in the ceremony, either just before or after the vows.

Butterflies

Indians believe that butterflies take silent wishes for the bride and groom to the heavens. This is very pretty when incorporated into an outdoor ceremony. Remember to take the butterflies out of the refrigerator in plenty of time so they are 'awake' and ready to take flight, otherwise you might have some comedic relief at your ceremony when the butterflies go nowhere.

Ribbon Ceremony/Handfasting

The ancient Celts of Ireland tied the hands of the bride and groom. The officiant loosely binds the hands together. They remain that way for the rest of the ceremony. A cord, ribbon, rosary, or scarf can be used.

Rose Ceremony

This is a symbolic ceremony using roses, the symbol of love. The couples who have chosen this give each other a rose as their first gift to each other. This is usually done right after the vows and ring exchange.

Families Service

Parents become part of the introduction to the vows. The officiant asks, "Who brings this couple to be wed?" and both of the parents either answer or have a moment to say something. This is a little different than the part where the Bride alone is given away.

The Lasso

This is a beautiful tradition where the bride and groom are linked together by a giant rosary that is loosely placed around them for most of the ceremony. You can be creative and use a garland of flowers, or even a beautiful rope or long scarf.

Wine or Water Ceremony

The couple shares a cup of wine or water while the officiant says a blessing and a reading. The

American Indians have a wedding container/vase with two drinking spouts. The bride drinks from one side and the groom drinks from the other side. This ceremony unites them into one.

Blessing to the Four Directions or Four Winds

At one time, people believed the human soul shared characteristics with all things celestial. This prayer service designates the four points on a compass (north, south, east and west) with human virtues. It is sometimes known as the Blessing of the Four Winds.

Jumping the Broom

This tradition has its roots in Africa and carried over to American Slavery. There are many different versions of this ritual, which involves the couple jumping over the broom usually near or at the end of the ceremony. The jumping of the broom is a symbol of sweeping away of the old and welcoming the new, or a symbol of a new beginning. It can also be used as a symbol of fertility and prosperity for the couple.

6

CEREMONY AND BLESSING WORDING SAMPLES

The following Ceremony and Blessing wordings are those used in Ceremonies I perform. They can easily be modified depending on the ceremony requirements. For example, if the outer individual candles during the Unity Candle ceremony is first being lit by the mothers, a wording can be added whereby the mothers are invited up to light the outer candles. Then the Bride and Groom are invited up to light the center candle.

Unity Candle

Lighting the Unity Candle is a symbol of the union created by a man and a woman who enter into marriage. They are no longer two, but one. It is written, "For this cause shall a man leave his father and mother, and shall cleave to his wife, and the two shall become one flesh." Three candles stand before you. The two outer candles represent the lives of _____ and _____ and their families who nurtured them in their beliefs.

Until now, _____ and _____ have let their light shine as individuals in their respective homes and communities. Today, as they light the center candle, they join their lights and their love in this new union as husband and wife. They do not lose their individuality, yet in marriage, they are united in so close a bond that they truly do become one in heart, mind and soul. A famous scholar once wrote: "From every human being there rises a light that reaches straight to heaven. And when two souls are destined to find one another, their two streams of light flow together, and a single brighter light goes forth from their united being." _____ and _____, as you jointly light your candle, it is our prayer that you will continually rekindle the candles of your love throughout your lives, so that there always will be light and joy, peace and harmony in your hearts and in your home.

Four Winds Blessing

O Great Spirit: Bless us from the North with the cool winds that calm our passions Bless us from the East with the winds that bring and renew life. Bless us from the South with the warm wet winds that invite growth. Bless us from the West with the winds that lead us through this life to the next. Fill the sky so that we may sense Your presence. And bless us from Mother Earth from which we have come and to whom we shall return.

Butterfly Release Ceremony - American Indian legend

If anyone desires a wish to come true they must first capture a butterfly and whisper that wish to it.

Since a butterfly can make no sound, the butterfly cannot reveal the wish to anyone but the Great Spirit who hears and sees all. In gratitude for giving the beautiful butterfly its freedom, the Great Spirit always grants the wish. So, according to legend, by making a wish and giving the butterfly its freedom, the wish will be taken to the heavens and be granted.

We have gathered to grant this couple all our best wishes and are about to set these butterflies free in trust that all these wishes will be granted.

Sample Poems to Honor the Deceased
You can ask a family member or a friend to read one of the following poems at some point during your ceremony.

Sample 1:
Although we can't see you
We know you are here
Smiling down, watching over us
As we say "I DO"
Forever in our hearts
Forever in our lives
And so we say our vows
In loving memory of you.

Sample 2:
Although death has separated us physically, faith and love have bound us eternally.
Though we cannot see you, we know you are here.

Though we cannot touch you, we feel the warmth of your smile, as we begin a new chapter in our lives. Today we pause to reflect upon those who have shaped our character, molded our spirits and touched our hearts.

May the lighting of this candle be a reminder of the memories we have shared, a representation of the everlasting impact you have made upon our lives.

Sample 3:
In Loving Memory of those who could
not be with us to share our special day
For those we have loved and lost along the way,
A flame to remember them burns here today.
For the laughter, smiles and memories remain,
Together today their presence sustains.
Never forgotten and loved forever more,
Today their blessings flicker and soar.

Wishing Stones

Before you met, your lives were on different paths with different destinations. But love has brought you together and joined these separate paths into one. Each one of your friends and family here today have been given a small polished stone that represents their unique individuality and their presence at your wedding today. You also each have a stone of your own that symbolizes your previous separate lives, separate sets of friends, separate families and the different life's journeys you once traveled.

I will now ask that everyone please take out the stone you have been given and pause to make a wish or blessing for happiness and good will for the couple for the future of their marriage.

After the ceremony we will follow _____ and _____to the water, and cast our stone into the water.

These wishing stones we will toss into the ocean symbolize the blessings and wishes to be never-ending as is the tide.

The ripples that are made represent the love and good wishes not only for _____ and _____, but for all of the world. As our ripples cross and re-cross one another's, so do our love and good wishes touch and retouch all around us.

As the stones are combined with love into the ocean, so now are your friends and family joined, through you, into one. And your once solitary life's paths are also now one. All that was once separate is now shared, and in this sharing you both will find new strength and joy as together you forge a new life's path and destination.

Starfish Ceremony

The starfish is the symbol for infinite love. Each of you has been given a starfish to hold, bless, and protect. _____ and _____ ask that you pray for infinite blessings for their marriage. After the ceremony, please join us at the water's edge as we cast these stars into the ocean and make a wish for a marriage full of infinite love.

Sand Ceremony

Today you've made a commitment to share the rest of your lives with each other. Your relationship is symbolized through the pouring together of these two individual containers of sand. _____, through the sands of time you have grown into the person you are today. This container of sand represents all that you were, all that you are, and all that you will ever be. _____, through the sands of time you have grown into the person you are today. This container of sand represents all that you were, all that you are, and all that you will ever be. As you each hold your separate container of sand, it symbolizes your lives prior to this moment, individual and unique. Now as you blend the sands together, it symbolizes the blending together of your two hands, two hearts, and two lives into one. (The sands are combined into the Unity Sand Bottle.) Just as these grains of sand can never be separated again, so may your lives be blended together for all Eternity.

Celebration of the New Family

When a couple marries, it is not just the joining of two lives together, it is the coming together of families as well. This is especially true today. For as _____ and _____ become husband and wife, they also are joined now by (children's names) to become a family. At this time, we recognize (children's names) and acknowledge their significance on this wedding day.

Rose Ceremony for Mothers

This wedding celebration is a joining of two unique families who stood separate until today. Today we unite these families by the marriage of _____ and _____. _____ and _____ would each like to honor the separateness of their families and now, the togetherness, with the giving of a rose to their mothers. They would also like to acknowledge the love and sacrifice that each mother has made to make their children who they are today - - a man and woman who are ready to be in a committed, loving marriage of their own. (Bride and Groom present a rose to their mothers)

Rose Ceremony – First Gift to Each Other

In a few moments you will receive the most honorable titles that exist between a man and a woman – the titles of husband and wife. You have chosen to give each other a rose as your first gift. In the language of flowers, the rose was considered a symbol of love, and a single rose meant only one thing – "I love you". So it is appropriate that your first gift to each other as husband and wife will be a single rose. Please exchange your gifts.

Because you both have given and received this symbol of love, I would encourage you to choose one very special place in your home for roses. Then on each anniversary, you both may take a rose to that special place as a recommitment to your marriage, and express with this symbol that your marriage is a marriage based on love.

In every marriage, there are times when it is difficult to verbalize certain feelings. Sometimes, we hurt those whom we love most, then find it difficult to say, "I am sorry," or "Please forgive me," or "I need you."

When you simply cannot find those words, leave a rose at your specially chosen place, and let that rose say what matters most ---"I still love you." The other should accept this rose for the words that cannot be found, and remember that the unspoken love is the hope you share and the faith you have in your future together as husband and wife

Blessing of the Rings

By Air, by Fire, by Water, and by Earth do I bless and consecrate these rings. (The Officiant may present the rings to each direction/element).

These rings, a token of your love for one another, serve as a reminder that all in life is a cycle; all comes to pass and passes away and comes to pass again.

May the element of Air bless these rings. Air is at the beginning of all things, the direction of East, and the dawning of a new day. May your lives through the reminder of this ring be blessed with continuing renewal of love. (*Waves rings through incense smoke*)

May the element of Fire bless these rings. Fire is the passion within your love, the spark of love itself, the heat of anger, and the warmth of compassion. It is the direction of South, the heat of midday. May your lives through the reminder of this ring be blessed with continual warmth. (*Passes the rings through flame*)

May the element of Water bless these rings. Water nourishes and replenishes us, the waters of emotion and harmony pour vitality into our lives. It is the direction of West, the afternoon and evening. May your lives through the reminder of this ring be blessed with fulfillment and contentment. (*Submerges the rings in water*)

May the element of Earth bless these rings. All life springs from the earth and returns to the earth, the direction of North, the nighttime. May your lives through the reminder of this ring be blessed with strength and solidity. (*Touches the rings to earth or a stone*)

May the Lord bless these rings, the symbol of union, with happiness, wholeness, and love. (optional)

I consecrate these rings with the element of Air, the breath of life. I consecrate these rings with the element of Fire for the warmth of love. I consecrate these rings with the element of Water to wash them clean. I consecrate these rings with the element of Earth for solidity and stability.

Air for hopes and dreams; Fire for the spark of love; Water for harmony and healing; and Earth for strength. May these rings be so Blessed.

Breaking of the Glass

In a few moments, we will conclude this ceremony with the Breaking of the Glass. In Jewish tradition, the breaking of the glass at a wedding is a symbolic prayer and hope that your love for one another will remain until the pieces of the glass come together again, or in other words, that your love will last forever. The fragile nature of the glass also suggests the frailty of human relationships. Even the strongest of relationships is subject to disintegration. The glass then, is broken to 'protect' the marriage with this implied prayer; May your bond of love be as difficult to break as it would be to put together again the pieces of this glass.

Four Winds Blessing

In times past it was believed that the human soul shared characteristics with all things divine. It is this belief which assigned virtues to the cardinal directions; East, South, West and North. It is in this tradition that a blessing is offered in support of this ceremony.

Blessed be this union with the gifts of the East. Communication of the heart, mind, and body;

Fresh beginnings with the rising of each Sun. The knowledge of the growth found in the sharing of silences.

Blessed be this union with the gifts of the South. Warmth of hearth and home; The heat of the heart's passion; The light created by both to lighten the darkest of times.

Blessed be this union with the gifts of the West. The deep commitments of the lake; The swift excitement of the river; The refreshing cleansing of the rain; The all encompassing passion of the sea.

Blessed be this union with the gifts of the North. Firm foundation on which to build; Fertility of the fields to enrich your lives; a stable home to which you may always return.

Each of these blessings from the four cardinal directions emphasizes those things which will help you build a happy and successful union. Yet they are only tools. Tools which you must use together in order to create what you seek in this union.

To make your marriage work will take Love. Love should be the core of your marriage; love is the reason you are here. But it also will take Trust – to know in your hearts you want the best for each other. It will take dedication – to stay open to one another; to learn and to grow together even when this is not always so easy to do. It will take Faith – to always be willing to go forward to tomorrow, never really knowing what tomorrow will bring. And it will take commitment – to hold true to the journey you both now pledge to share together.

Handfasting

Please look at your hands and turn your palms up so you may see the blessing they are to you. Now hold each other's hands, right hand to right hand and left hand to left hand forming the symbol of eternity. _____ and _____, this cord is a symbol of the life you have chosen to live together. You once were separate in thought, word and deed, but as this cord is tied together, so shall your lives become intertwined. (Tie cord) With this cord, I bind you to the vows that you have made to one another. With this knot, I tie you heart to heart, together as one.

The knot of this binding is not bound by the cord, but rather by your own vows of love. For, as always, you hold in your own hands the making or breaking of this union. May this "love knot" always be a reminder of the binding together of two hands, two hearts, and two souls into one. And so are you bound, each to the other, for all the days of your lives. (Remove cord)

Handfasting 2

As this knot is tied, so are your lives now bound. Woven into this cord, imbued into its very fibers, are all the hopes of your friends and family, and of yourselves, for your new life together. With the fashioning of this knot do I tie all the desires, dreams, love, and happiness wished here in this place to your lives for as long as love shall last. In the joining of hands and the fashion of a knot, so are your lives now bound, one to another. By this cord you are thus bound to your vow. May this knot remain tied for as long as love shall last. May this cord draw your hands together in love, never to be used in anger. May the vows you have spoken never grow bitter in your mouths.

As any child discovers when they are learning to tie their own shoes, the first move is to cross the ends. The cross creates the Rune Gebo (X), which is the

Rune of partnership and union. As your hands are bound by this cord, so is your partnership held by the symbol of this knot. May it be granted that what is done before the gods be not undone by man.

Two entwined in love, bound by commitment and fear, sadness and joy, by hardship and victory, anger and reconciliation, all of which brings strength to this union. Hold tight to one another through both good times and bad, and watch as your strength grows.

Apache Wedding Blessing

Now you will feel no rain, for each of you will be shelter for the other. Now you will feel no cold, for each of you will be warmth to the other. Now there will be no loneliness, for each of you will be companion to the other. Now you are two persons, but there is only one life before you. May beauty surround you both in the journey ahead and through all the years, May happiness be your companion and your days together be good and long upon the earth.

Treat yourselves and each other with respect, and

remind yourselves often of what brought you together. Give the highest priority to the tenderness, gentleness and kindness that your connection deserves. When frustration, difficult and fear assail your relationship - as they threaten all relationships at one time or another - remember to focus on what is right between you, not only the part which seems wrong. In this way, you can ride out the storms when clouds hide the face of the sun in your lives - remembering that even if you lose sight of it for a moment, the sun is still there. And if each of you takes responsibility for the quality of your life together, it will be marked by abundance and delight.

Cherokee Wedding Blessing

Father Sky please protect the ones we love.
We honor all you created as we pledge our hearts and lives together.
We honor Mother Earth - and ask for our marriage to be abundant and grow stronger through the seasons;
We honor fire - and ask that our union be warm and glowing with love in our hearts;
We honor wind - and ask we sail though life safe

and calm as in our father's arms;
We honor water - to clean and soothe our
relationship - that it may never thirst for love;
With all the forces of the universe you created, we
pray for harmony and true happiness as we forever
grow young together.

Navajo Wedding Blessing

Now you have lit a fire and that fire should not go
out. The two of you now have a fire that represents
love, understanding and a philosophy of life. It will
give you heat, food, warmth and happiness. The
new fire represents a new beginning - a new life and
a new family. The fire should keep burning; you
should stay together. You have lit the fire for life,
until old age separates you.

Hand Ceremony

Always remember these are the hands of your best
friend that are full of love today as you promise
yourselves to each other, that will work alongside
yours as you build your future together, that will
comfort you like no other. These are the hands that
will give you strength when you struggle and
encouragement to chase down your dreams. They

will tenderly hold your children and help keep your family together as one. These hands you hold today will countless times, wipe the tears from your eyes, tears of sorrow and tears of joy. And lastly, these are the hands, that even when wrinkled with age, will still be reaching for yours, still giving you the same unspoken tenderness and love with just a touch.

7

READINGS

Since this book was written as an educational resource for people planning a wedding, it wouldn't be complete without a section on Readings. In addition to the Vows, the Readings that are chosen will make a Ceremony even more personal. All of the readings listed in this Chapter have been given to me frequently by Brides and Grooms for inclusion in their Ceremony. While trying to identify who wrote these works, and provide information about the Authors, I was surprised at how widely used and openly available they are on the Internet. In no particular order, the most used by my clients are: The Art of Marriage by Wilferd

A. Peterson, This Day I Married My Best Friend (author unknown), I Promise by Dorothy R. Colgan, Oh, The Places You'll Go by Dr. Seuss, Union by Robert Fulghum and Corinthians 1-13 (Modern Version). HINT: What a great idea it would be (and one I think is very special, different, and personal) is to purchase the book your selected reading is in and give it to your partner as a wedding gift. Another suggestion is to buy it as a special present for your first Anniversary and write a private note inside expressing your love.

The Art of Marriage by Wilferd A. Peterson - NOTE: This is great for a wedding and vow renewal ceremony. It's meaningful in its entirety and is one of my favorites. The full version is available on Amazon.com. Book title is: *The Art of Marriage* by Wilferd A. Peterson

This Day I Married My Best Friend (author unknown)

I Promise by Dorothy R. Colgan - NOTE: Some couples 'share' the reading with each other alternating the I promise sections i.e. Bride reads the first I promise verse, Groom reads the second I promise verse with both reading the last I promise verse together.

Never Marry But For Love by William Penn

Marriage Joins Two People in the Circle of its Love by Edmund O'Neill

Dove Poem
(author unknown)

To Be One With Each Other by George Eliot

Marriage Is the Closest Kind of Friendship by Nicholas Gordon

Excerpts from the *Velveteen Rabbit* by Margery Williams

Foundations of Marriage by Regina Hill

A Time to Laugh by Joan Chittister

The Story of a Tree excerpted from *The Legacy of Luna* by Julia Butterfly Hill

I Like You by Sandol Stoddard Warburg – NOTE: This was originally written as a children's book but is so very cute when read at a wedding. The more animated and enthusiastic your reader is the better. Your guests will love it.

To Love is Not to Possess by James Kavanaugh

Yes, I'll Marry You by Pam Ayres

Carrie's Poem from Sex and the City

Various excerpts from *The Prophet* by Kahlil Gilbran

Union by Robert Fulghum - NOTE: This is a beautiful piece and one of my very favorites. It should be read only in its entirety. It makes for an amazingly touching introduction to the vows. It is contained in a book: *From Beginning to End – The Rituals of Our Lives* by Robert Fulghum

Love Is Friendship Caught Fire by Laura Hendricks

I Love You by Roy Croft

I carry your heart with me by e.e. cummings – NOTE: This was featured in the movie 'In Her Shoes' and was read by Cameron Diaz at her sisters wedding.

Oh, The Places You'll Go by Dr. Seuss - NOTE: This is really cute when done with enthusiasm. It'll add a lot to your ceremony. The full version is available on Amazon.com. Book title is: *Oh, The Places You'll Go* by Dr. Seuss.

Love credited to Ann Landers

Sonnet XLIII by Elizabeth Barrett Browning

Marriage Joins Two People in the Circle of its Love by Edmund O'Neill

Sooner or Later (author unknown)

There are numerous variations of Corinthians 1-13. The most popular is the Modern Version, followed by the International, New Living and English Standard Versions. One website all versions can be found at is www.biblegateway.com as well as from the Catholic and King James Bibles.

8

DON'T FORGET

It's your wedding day and you are bound to forget something. Please use the following list as a helpful reminder. It is spaced in such a way that you can make notes.

For Her:

Rings

License

Hand Lotion, Wet Wipes

Curling Iron, hot rollers

Tissues

Hair dryer

Cotton balls, cotton swabs

Brush, comb

Make up

Hairspray, hair gel

Make up remover

Bobby pins, clips, barrettes

Nail polish in shade worn

Headband to hold your hair back

Clear nail polish for runs

Toothbrush, toothpaste, floss

Extra pantyhose

Lint brush/tape

Nail polish remover

Baby powder

Nail file

Deodorant

Tweezers

Perfume

Small grooming scissors or kit

Small hand towel

Safety pins, sewing kit, scissors, extra buttons

Tampax/sanitary pads

Stain removal solutions

Extra earring backs

Iron or steam iron

Flat shoes for the reception

Bandages

Antacid

Upset stomach remedy

Prescription meds

Small flashlight

Aspirin/pain relievers

Folding utility knife

Directions to reception/extra copies

Duct tape

Breath mints

Cooler with juice, sodas, bottled water

Phone numbers for all of the wedding party

Munchies

Contact information for all vendors

Writing pen

Reading glasses

Matches/Lighter

Small writing pad

For Him:

Black Socks (an extra pair)

Brush, comb

Cologne (travel size)

Corsage pins

Extra shirt buttons

Extra cufflinks

Handkerchiefs

Lint brush

Sewing kit, buttons, needle

Safety pins, straight pins

Shoe polish

Spot remover

Wrinkle out spray

Duct tape

Directions to reception (extra copies)

Phone numbers of family, wedding party

Vendor contact numbers

Notebook and pens

Portable flashlight

Change (quarters in case)

Snacks (granola, fruit, bottled water, juice)

Umbrella

Watch

Matches/Lighter

Antacid

Aspirin, pain reliever

Band aids

Reading glasses, contact lenses, lens solution

Deodorant

Eye-drops

Insect repellent (make sure it smells nice)

Lotion

Medications

Mints

Moist towelettes

Mouthwash

Sunscreen

Toothbrush and toothpaste

Tissues

Wash cloth or hand towel

Cash ($20 or more)

Tips for vendors

Cell phone (remember to turn it off)

Disposable camera

Driver's license or photo ID card

9

HIRING A DJ

By now, you've probably read numerous magazines, seen television shows, and surfed the net for websites that tell you what you need for your perfect wedding. Have you noticed though your entertainment is one of the last items mentioned, if it's mentioned at all? I can't begin to tell you how many brides or grooms call three, two, and yes even one week before their wedding date looking for a Disc Jockey who is inexpensive. Well, toss away anything you've read or heard about hiring a wedding DJ because here is what you need to know from a wedding entertainment specialist's point of view.

I have a question for you first… How many of you has ever seen an appetizer get a group of people up to dance, or seen a centerpiece make that first introduction of a married couple? If your answer is never, then why is it the food and flowers are purchased long before the entertainment is thought of.   I've had brides call and tell me they've spent $150 or more per person for an elegant dinner for their guests, yet with these outrageous prices for a salad and a piece of rosemary chicken, adding a mere $10 or $15 per head for entertainment is too much. I hope by now you get where I'm going with this.

When you look back at weddings you've attended, what was it that was the driving force in how the evening went. What held your guests attention? What kept your guests entertained and there? Was it the décor and flowers or the food?

It IS the entertainment that pulls your reception together, keeps your guests entertained and makes for some fantastic photos.

So, here's your first lesson: when you decide to get married, besides booking your wedding venue first, book your DJ then start looking around for the most reasonable dinner and flowers you can find, not the cheapest DJ at the last minute.

Which brings me to the next item – Pricing and DJ standards. When you start calling around for prices, you'll probably be easily confused because while there are no standards for pricing, there are also no standards for who calls themselves a DJ. I want to repeat this last part, there are NO standards for who calls themselves a DJ. Some DJ's even try to dazzle you with terms like "DMX lighting" as a cover. Let's see if I can't clarify some of this for you.

A good DJ will spend 20 or more hours putting together and preparing your wedding reception before they show up on that special day. They will take the time getting to know you and take the time getting to know what you want. Your reception should be personalized to fit you, not a canned performance everyone gets. While it's fun to fill out a planning form on a website, you need to ask yourself if your DJ is really going to know you, and what you want. Halls and Salons frequently use a 'house DJ' and receive some type of monetary compensation. The DJ who is there isn't always the best fit for you. Remember, your DJ (and venue) works for you and is there to make your day what you've dreamed of. You should be comfortable with your DJ and comfortable with the trust you place in him/her. If it doesn't feel right; don't do it no matter what kind of a deal you think you are getting or how professional it seems or cool it is to fill out forms on a website. (Everyone else is filling out the same form.) Meet with your DJ including house or package-everything-included DJ's and get to know him/her. Watch for their passion for what they do and their interest in making your day YOU.

You DO only have this day once and your entertainment can make it or break it. If your DJ isn't willing to put in the time to make your day reflect your personality, likes and dislikes; isn't available to meet with you; doesn't return your calls; doesn't call you just to check in; then I would run the other way. When there is a House DJ, make your own DJ selection part of your contract before you sign the contract. You shouldn't be penalized or charged an extra fee for wanting your day perfect. If you are, either negotiate or look elsewhere.

You might get a warm and fuzzy feeling from the DJ you've interviewed but so very many times, especially with bigger companies called multi-ops, you'll talk with one person and someone entirely different shows up. You don't know if that person is a rookie DJ with YOUR wedding being his/her first as often happens or an experienced professional. If your DJ says they are sending or might send someone else, meet with that person BEFORE you sign your contract and have it put in your contract that will be the person who will show up. I get calls frequently from other DJ's I've never met looking for someone to cover a wedding. You are the one calling the shots, not your DJ, so ask the questions. If you aren't satisfied with the answers, keep running.

Is it really a business….. ? There are so many DJ's out there who don't run a "legitimate" business. At the very least, your DJ should have liability insurance, have their business registered in the state they operate out of, have a contract/agreement outlining the performance terms that protects both the DJ and you, and get their music from a legitimate source (and NOOOO, downloading music from the internet even if you pay for it isn't legal when used for paid performances). Belonging to professional organizations such as the National Association of Mobile Entertainers (NAME) is a plus because they hold their members to a higher standard. Holding any other certifications is a real added bonus because you know they take their profession seriously enough to work at it. I know DJ's who've been in the business for 15 or 20 years and have never been to a training conference and don't receive any professional publications. I've also seen their performances...dull and stagnant are two words that come to mind. So you might want to ask how your DJ is keeping current with the changes, laws, rules and regulations in the entertainment industry not to mention the equipment.

O.K. I know you've probably been asking "What IS DMX lighting?" since I mentioned it. Well, don't be impressed by terminology or the DJ's who throw it around without explaining what it is. There are basically three types of lights 1) turn it on and it does its own thing 2) turn it on and it beats or flashes to the music or 3) turn it on and you tell it what to do. This is called DMX lighting and requires programming. Every venue and set of lights needs its own programming to be complimentary to the room and the event AND there are very few DJ's who can program lighting at the event (on the fly). DMX lighting also beats and flashes to the music. So while your DJ says they HAVE DMX lighting, ask them if they are going to program the lighting at your event and if you can watch. My guess is you will have DMX capable lighting that beats and flashes to the music. Your DJ should have professional grade equipment built for and used in the DJ industry so ask what they are using and if they bought it specifically to DJ with or at a local discount or drug store.

All of the above adds up to the professionalism and standards of the DJ you are hiring for your wedding day. It also adds into the price you will pay. One thing you need to remember: The day after your wedding, no one will be wearing a price-tag. Either you will have had a great time or you won't. The

day after your wedding is too late when you've made the wrong choice solely on price on the most special day of your life. You can't go back!

The current national average price for a 4 hour wedding reception is $1400. Prices range anywhere from $600 to well over $3500. Of course, there's always the friend of the family who has an IPOD/MP3 player who will do it for $300 but you have to ask yourself if it's worth it (see next article.) The cheapest isn't always the best choice for this once in a lifetime milestone and conversely the most expensive doesn't mean you've hired the best. An IPOD/MP3 player is just a tool. It's like using disposable cameras instead of hiring a photographer or serving fast food instead of having your reception catered.

What else? A good DJ should be able to emcee as well as DJ. If your wedding is longer than 5 hours or large you should consider asking your DJ to bring a second person if they haven't suggested it during your interview. This will keep the party energy level high and will add an additional touch of class and elegance. It might cost a little more but well worth it. Wireless microphones are fairly standard these days and you shouldn't have to pay extra for them. You might have to pay a small amount extra for a second sound system for your ceremony or cocktail area and for upgraded lighting (but not extra for DMX unless they are programming especially for you). Your DJ should be willing to take requests and willing to work with you on what you do and don't want to hear at your reception.

Finally, ask the questions. Make sure you hire someone who fits you, who will show up, and who is a professional with a legitimate business. Don't hire your entertainment last and look for the cheapest deal. Put your entertainment among the first things you look for when planning your wedding, then cut back on the number of roses in the centerpieces. Your guests probably won't remember the flowers or the Rosemary chicken but they WILL remember the entertainment. So will you.

10

MP3 Players vs. Professional DJs

I have read several articles encouraging Brides wishing to save a few dollars on their wedding, to use an MP3 player instead of hiring professional entertainment such as a Disc Jockey (DJ). The assumption that an MP3 player is all any reception needs shows complete lack of knowledge of the wedding industry and sets up the bridal couple to have their once in a lifetime day completely ruined. Long after it's forgotten how much everything cost, how much the photographer was paid or how many courses the meal was, the reception memories will still be there. They are permanent and will never be erased.

Think about all the receptions you've gone to. What do you remember? The centerpieces? The tablecloths? The Fun? I'll bet if you've ever heard bad entertainment that you don't remember the name of the group or DJ, but you do remember where you were when you heard it. Do you want the lasting memories of your reception to be where your guests (who gave you gifts) were entertained by an MP3 player pre-loaded with songs you like (and they've probably never heard of) or by a fantastic experienced professional DJ who can read the crowd and intertwine what you like with what will get your guests feet moving.

All of the industry experts I know agree there are no second chances to capture a once in a lifetime moment.

Brides hire professional photographers to make sure their special day is captured in time. Think about those cherished wedding albums. The first half contains posed pictures while the second half of the album has photos of people having fun. Action photos of bouquets being thrown, loving looks during the first dance, a father's wistful smile as he has his last dance with his daughter, friends linking arms and 'high kicking' to a special song, and special photos of guests dancing the night away as they celebrate

THERE IS NO MP3 PLAYER THAT WILL PROVIDE THE AMMUNITION FOR THESE PHOTOS. It's the professional DJ who does it.

An MP3 player is to a professional DJ as a disposable camera is to a professional photographer as fast food is to having the reception catered.

Consider this. If the meal is late or not what it should be, the professional DJ will get your guests minds off of it. If the photographer needs a special shot, the professional DJ will set it up. If there are any special announcements, the professional DJ will make them. If it's time to toss the bouquet or cut the cake or dance with the parents, the professional DJ will make sure the timing is right for the most impact. If Uncle Bert wants to hear a special song, the professional DJ will play it.

THERE IS NO MP3 PLAYER THAT CAN DO THIS.

As industry professionals, professional DJ's should be paid as much as photographers or as much as caterers, but they rarely are. Brides have been known to pay $7-$9 per guest for a piece of cake and another $3.00 to have it cut and served, but they think it's horrible to pay just a little more than that for entertainment. Yet it's the entertainment both the bride and their guests will remember; not the cake or who cut it.

Until a photographer or a centerpiece or an appetizer can get a group of people up to dance, an experienced, professional DJ is worth every dollar they are paid. There are ways to cut costs at a wedding, but using a MP3 player and eliminating a key professional who is essential to the success of a reception and contributes so much to permanent memories just sets up this "once in a lifetime moment" for complete disaster.

So I'll ask once again; What do you want YOUR guests to remember about YOUR reception?

I close this book like I started it.

I have the best job in the world. I am a Wedding Officiant. Enjoy each other and have a wonderful life together.

   --Cheryl Q

ABOUT THE BOOK AUTHOR

Wedding Officiant Dr. Cheryl Quinlan (Rev. Cheryl Q) of Fun Florida Weddings and A Vow Forever has been celebrating marriages since 2004 and is well-known for creating personalized ceremonies for couples. She is both a non-denominational minister (Doctor of Divinity) as well as a Notary authorized to perform Civil Ceremonies. She specializes in: Non-denominational, Religious, Inter-faith, Spiritual, and Civil ceremonies, Vow Renewals, Destination Weddings, Family Unions, and Commitment Ceremonies.

"Small or large, indoors or outside, it is my honor to preside over your Marriage."

Visit us at: www.avowforever.com
www.funfloridaweddings.com
www.facebook.com/funfloridaweddings